W9-BJT-395

DISCARDED

Property of
The Public Library of Nashville and Davidson County
225 Polk Ave., Nashville, Tn. 37203

DISCARDED

VISIONS
OF GOD
FROM THE
NEAR DEATH
EXPERIENCE

VISIONS OF GOD

FROM THE
NEAR DEATH EXPERIENCE

BY KEN R. VINCENT

PUBLISHED FOR THE PAUL BRUNTON
PHILOSOPHIC FOUNDATION BY

LARSON PUBLICATIONS

Copyright © 1994 by Ken R. Vincent

All rights are reserved. No part of this publication may be repro-
duced, stored in a retrieval system, or transmitted, in any form or by
any means, electronic, chemical, optical, photocopying, recording, or
otherwise without prior permission in writing from the publisher.

International Standard Book Number (cloth): 0-943914-66-3
International Standard Book Number (paper): 0-943914-67-1
Library of Congress Catalog Card Number: 93-81341

Published for the Paul Brunton Philosophic Foundation
by Larson Publications
4936 NYS Route 414
Burdett, NY 14818 USA

99   98   97   96   95   94

10 9 8 7 6 5 4 3 2 1

Grateful acknowledgement is made for permission to reprint from:

"Amazing Grace" K. Ring, *Journal of Near Death Studies,* © 1991,
10(1). By permission of Human Sciences Press.

Beyond Death's Door, M. Rawlings (© 1978). By permission of
Thomas Nelson, Inc.

Heading Toward Omega, K. Ring. Text copyright © 1984 by
Kenneth Ring. Ill. copyright © 1984. By permission of William
Morrow & Company, Inc.

Life After Life (© 1975) and *Reflections on Life After Life* (© 1977),
R. Moody. By permission of Mockingbird Books Inc.

The Light Beyond, R. Moody (© 1988). By permission of Bantam
Books.

Return from Death, M. Grey (© 1985). By permission of Penguin
Books Ltd.

Contents

Prologue		7
Chapter 1	*Introduction*	9
Chapter 2	*The Direct Experience of God*	19
Chapter 3	*Jesus*	45
Chapter 4	*Angels, Spirits, Deceased Loved Ones, and Other Helpers*	61
Chapter 5	*Judgment* (The Life Review)	77
Chapter 6	*After Effects*	97
Chapter 7	*Hell*	115
Chapter 8	*Theology*	133
Chapter 9	*What Is Required of Us*	143
Chapter 10	*Conclusions*	161
Epilogue		164
Notes to Chapter 1		165
References		166
Sources of Religious Quotations		168

To God

Who Makes Everything Possible

Prologue

I do not know if religion is true or heaven a place,
But this I know—at the end of the day
   God is revealed
And there for one brief moment one can see
   God and look through all eternity.
So when I die—
Look for me on the brink of twilight,
Gazing into the starry bliss of everlasting light.

CHAPTER 1

Introduction

Since the publication of Dr. Raymond Moody's classic book *Life After Life* in 1975, interest has continued to escalate on the Near Death Experience. A recent publication lists more than seven hundred references on the near death experience with most of the references being from scientific sources.[1] To sum up the results of this ongoing research to date is difficult at best, but it seems fair to say that while the near death experience appears to be related to other mystical experiences, it is not due to any known medical or psychological cause. In other words, it is not just due to a hallucination, or surgery, or drowning, or drugs, etc.

Recent research has focused on whether this unique cluster of symptoms is experienced by people who were not near death, but only thought they were. In a study reported in the medical journal *The Lancet*, Owens, Cook and Stevenson report that the unique feature in the experience of those who were actually clinically dead was that they were much more apt to experience enhanced perception of the Light and enhanced cognitive powers.[2] Citing primarily the brain mapping experiments of neurosurgeon Dr. Wilder Penfield, Dr. Melvin Morse states that much of the phenomenon of the near death experience appears to be experienced in the right temporal lobe of the brain—with the notable exception of the Light. It is this Light or Being of Light, which many experiencers go on to label God or an emissary of God, that is the subject of this book.

Whatever insights near death experiences may give us about an afterlife, they also and most importantly provide us with a generic vision of how humans see God. As with other mystical experiences of God, the experience is ineffable, that is, beyond words.

When near death experiencers try to talk about their experience, they are like individuals who have barely learned to speak a foreign language; they appear to be translating as they speak. Like all great truths, the truth of religious revelation is purest at the source. The vision of God from near death experiencers is much more consistent than the culturally embellished and theologically reworked visions of God from major religious works. Most religious views of afterlife appear to be culturally embellished versions of this common experience.

We have heard this story before, many times. In *The Tibetan Book of the Dead,* a twelfth-century Buddhist work, we are instructed to go to the Light, which is universal, but we are also told that the beings we see will correspond to the gods of our religion. Similarly, the five-thousand-year-old *Egyptian Book of the Dead* tells of going through the darkness and coming forth into the light. Indeed, the ancient Egyptian name for this book is *Coming Forth into the Day* or *Coming Forth into the Light*.

In this book the radiant being is a loving god, the original dying and rising god, Osiris, the King of After-life. It is he who "judges" our life. (This judging corresponds, in near death experience terminology, to the term "life review.") In the Christian view the judge is Jesus and in Islam the judge is God. The vision of God never changes, but the religious interpretation does. While near death experiencers give remarkably similar descriptions of the Being of Light, some do label the Being of Light as a particular religious figure.

Tom Harpur, a former Anglican priest, notes in an article in *Maclean's* that the near death experience, instead of being an attempt to deal with death, "is an attempt to express what has already become known, through direct experience."[3] Like other mystical experiences, near death experiences often profoundly change the lives of those who have them. Near death experiences are remarkably similar regardless of the culture, beliefs, or mode of death of the experiencer.

While the focus of this book is the experience of God which is manifest in the near death experience via the Being of Light, let us briefly look at two other types of religious revelation via mystical experience. These two types are: 1) the involuntary mystical experience, which the psychologist Abraham Maslow called "peak experiences," and 2) the sought-after mystical experience, which the physician and psychologist William James called the "cultivated mystical experience."[4]

The best known involuntary mystical experiences are the experience Moses had at the burning bush and

Jesus' experience of baptism. These examples of involuntary mysticism are limited, however, because we do not have a complete personal description of the individual's perception and feelings at the time. All we have is a religious reference that the experiences happened.

It is also very important to recognize that ordinary people have involuntary mystical experiences. In his book *The Meditative Mind,* for example, Dr. Daniel Goleman notes that a mid-70s poll asked the question, "Have you ever had the feeling of being very close to a powerful spiritual force that seemed to lift you out of yourself?".[5] "Forty percent," Goleman reports, "replied that it had happened at least once; twenty percent said that it had happened several times; and five percent reported that it had happened often. Almost all of these people confessed they had never spoken to anyone— therapist, minister, priest, or rabbi—about their experiences. 'They would think I was crazy' was the reason. Such experiences do not fit in with the Western worldview or religious worldview, let alone the psychological worldview. As a nation of 'closet mystics' our theories of human possibility are, as a whole, very limited. We have a collective blind spot."

The situation is further complicated, as William James noted, by the fact that "This incommunicableness of the transport is the keynote of all mysticism. Mystical truth exists for the individual who has the transport, but for no one else."[6]

From a scientific perspective, the major problem in

studying involuntary mystical experiences is the anecdotal nature of the data. In a recent study in the *Journal of Nervous and Mental Disease*, researchers using the language that individuals use to describe the altered status of mysticism, schizophrenia, and drug states as well as statements of everyday personal experiences, were able to demonstrate via factor analysis that the language of these experiences does not overlap.[7] This indicates that these states are more different than alike. Quite simply, mental illness and mysticism are not related.

Now let us go on to explore the second type of religious revelation, cultivated or sought-after mystical experience. William James noted that "Hindus, Buddhists, Moslems and Christians have all cultivated mysticism methodically," via meditation.[8] In *The Meditative Mind*, Dr. Daniel Goleman analyzes twelve types of meditation from a variety of religions and notes that the levels and states described in all of them are similar.[9] To quote the Sufi Abu Said of Mineh, "The way to God is but one step; the step out of yourself." Or to quote Jesus in the *Gospel of Thomas* ". . . the angels and the prophets will come to you and give you those things that you already have." The sought-after path to religious revelation is via the mystical experience through a primary pathway of meditation. Meditation is the common link among Moses, Buddha, Zarathushtra, Jesus, Mohammed, and all other great religious leaders.

Think of it: What did Moses do on Mount Sinai? We don't know exactly, but he was gone a long time before

God came to him with the ten commandments—long enough for the Hebrews to think he was dead and to build the Golden Calf. Unfortunately, what we usually have in mind is Cecil B. DeMille's image of Moses anxiously waiting for God, but meditation seems more plausible.

The description of Jesus in the wilderness is also sketchy, but he was there for forty days, which is Bible talk for a long time.

In the *Zend Avesta*, the holy book of the Magi and of modern Pharsees, the prophet Zarathushtra—who also sought God in the wilderness—states: "Then did I realize Thee as the Most Bountiful One, O God, when the Good Mind encircled me completely. God declared to me that silent meditation is the best for attaining spiritual enlightenment."

Buddha, we know, sought enlightenment via meditation while sitting under a Bo tree. More recently, and with more detail, we know that Mohammed meditated in a cave until one day God, via the angel Gabriel, came to him with the Koran.

To the mystic, mystical revelation is open to *all* who seek it. The Christian nun and the Buddhist monk experience what we call God just as the prophets did, but in some cases this takes years of discipline and is something that happens only rarely. What makes the prophets different is that they were able to convince others of their mystical revelations.

The contribution of the near death experience to religious revelation is that while these experiences have occurred from time immemorial, especially to drowning victims, they now happen frequently, thanks to modern resuscitation techniques. According to George Gallup, several million Americans have had the near death experience. We now have thousands of individual accounts of this phenomenon. And even though most are as reluctant to talk about them as individuals are who have had other mystical experiences,[10] those that have come forth with their accounts report a remarkably consistent story of God, peace, and love experienced first-hand.

But what of the personality of the mystical experiencer? William James separated the mystical experience into religious mysticism and diabolical mysticism. The latter he identified with the mentally ill. He felt the two types were different but could not explain why. In the past few years, medical and psychological research has occasionally focused on this topic. In 1980, for example, the *Diagnostic and Statistical Manual of Mental Disorders III* of the American Psychiatric Association came out and said that it was alright for God to talk to you.[11] This obviously was not due to religious conversion but rather to evidence supporting a frank admission that mystical states are different from psychosis and drug-induced hallucinations. Research on individuals having mystical experiences does, in fact, relate mysticism to positive mental health on a variety of personality tests measuring mental health. I quote Maslow's research on the subject as an example: "... it has also been discovered that precisely those persons who have the clearest and strongest identity are exactly the ones who are most able to transcend the ego or the self and to become selfless . . ."[12]

Here again, the near death experience has something to add because it is an event that happens to people from the general population. Eighty percent of the general population and, correspondingly, eighty percent of near death experiencers are normal or mentally healthy.

Visions of God coming from the near death experience have two other important things to add to our knowledge of God via direct religious revelation. First is the *consistency* of the revelations which are taken from many people from different cultures, ethnic groups, and religious training. Second is the closeness to the source of the revelation. Using the Biblical Christian gospels as an example, we have four different accounts of the life and teachings of Jesus. Also we know that these gospels were reworked and edited prior to the second century.[13] Nevertheless, when we read at least the first three gospels and don't pick at them, we do get a flavor of who Jesus was and of his message of God.

Which brings us to the methodology of this book. The overwhelming majority of the cases in this book are first-hand accounts from experiencers as told in their own words, and taken from my own cases or the literature. A few are second-hand accounts from reliable sources that are included because of their poignant but nevertheless consistent nature. Sources for all are referenced if they are not my own. Finally, it is worth noting that many of my cases have come from a support group for near death experiencers led by my friend, Pam Kircher, M.D., at Unity Church of Christianity. I am a member of God's more skeptical denomination, the Unitarians. Nevertheless, I have come to believe that the vision of God from the near death experience is our cleanest and most generic vision of God. This makes perfect sense, for if God gets personal with us all, where else would we all find God, but on the brink of twilight.

With regard to the structure of this book, all quotations on the left-hand pages are from religious and literary sources listed in the Religious Quotations section which follows the References section at the end of the text. Sources for near death experiences, which appear on right-hand pages, are referenced as follows:

All references notated with a case number, for example *Case 1,* are the author's own. For all others, see the Reference section for complete citations of sources. All near death experiences that occurred in childhood are noted as "NDE" and include the experiencer's age at that time.

All Biblical quotations are from the New Revised Standard Version.

CHAPTER 2

The Direct Experience
of God

I am ascending to my Father
and your Father,
to my God and your God.

Jesus (John 20:17)

It seemed like God was there.

—*Case 1*, NDE age 10

I left my body and I was surrounded by God.
I didn't feel male or female, young or old, just me.
I was surrounded by love . . .
I looked down at the little girl in the bed . . .
Later when I realized it was me I was back
in my body.

—*Case 12*, NDE age 5

Now I know there's a God and that God is
everything that exists, [that's] the essence of
God. . . . Everything that exists has the essence
of God within it. I know there's a God now.
I have no question.

—*Heading Toward Omega*

. . . a beautiful experience with God, it changed
my life.

—*Case 8*, NDE age 4

Blessed are the pure in heart,
for they will see God.

Jesus (Matthew 5:8)

I understood that Being is truly multidimensional and oh so much bigger than any label we can come up with—and therefore, so must God be.

—*Love and God in the Near Death Experience*

And deep within me came an instant and wondrous recognition: I, *even I,* was facing God.

—*Amazing Grace*

. . . we are aspects of the one perfect whole, and as such are part of God, and of each other.

—*Amazing Grace*

God was really cool!

—*The Return from Silence*

We came from the light . . .

Jesus (Gospel of Thomas v.50)

. . . I looked up and saw an incredible light—
crystal-clear and brighter than the sun, but you
could look right into it without hurting your
eyes. Inside the light was the figure of a man
with his hand held out to me, radiating so much
love. It was the most beautiful feeling I've ever
experienced. I never wanted to leave.

—*At Death's Window*

I was in the light for a long time. It seemed like
a long time. I felt everyone loved me there.
Everyone was happy. I feel that the light
was God.

—*The Light Beyond*

To the Divine Body of Truth,
the Incomprehensible,
Boundless Light . . .

Opening to
The Tibetan Book of the Dead

I was in the universe and I was Light. It takes all the fear of dying out of you. It was heavenly. I was in the presence of God.

—*Case 14*

An absolute white Light that is God—all loving. The reunification of us with our creator.

—*Case 12*

I went directly into The Light, and my pain ceased. There was a feeling of extreme peace.

—*Case 25*

I came into the arc of pure golden love and light. This radiation of love entered me and instantly I was part of it and it was part of me.

—*Return from Death*

God's Body is Light . . . .

Zarathushtra

It's something which becomes you and you become it. I could say, "I was peace, I was love." I was the brightness, it was part of me . . .

—*Heading Toward Omega*

It was just pure consciousness. And this enormously bright light seemed almost to cradle me. I just seemed to exist in it and be part of it and be nurtured by it and the feeling just became more and more ecstatic and glorious and perfect.

—*Heading Toward Omega*

I was going toward the light, and told them to stop reviving me. I did not want to be revived.

—*Case 2*

Coming Forth into the Light

Original title of

The Egyptian Book
of the Dead

It was neither a man nor a woman, but it was both. I have never, before or since, seen anything as beautiful, loving, and perfectly pleasant as this being. An immense, radiant love poured from it. An incredible light shone through every single pore of its face. The colors of the light were magnificent, vibrant and alive. The light radiated outward. It was a brilliant white superimposed with what I can only describe as a golden hue. I was filled with an intense feeling of joy and awe. I was consumed with an absolutely inexpressible amount of love. I had the overpowering feeling that I was in the presence of the source of my life and perhaps even my creator. In spite of the tremendous awe it inspired, I felt I knew this being extremely well. With all my heart I wanted to embrace and melt into it as if we were one—for although it was neither my mother nor my father, it was both.

—*Heading Toward Omega*

The seekers of the light are one.

Samuel Longfellow

Upon entering that light . . . the atmosphere,
the energy, it's total pure energy, it's total
knowledge, it's total love, pure love—everything
about it is definitely the afterlife, if you will.

—*Heading Toward Omega*

As I reached the source of the light I could see
in. I cannot begin to describe in human terms
the feeling I had at what I saw. It was a giant
infinite world of calm, and love, and energy
and beauty.

—*Heading Toward Omega*

There was a brilliant golden light, and I don't
remember feeling frightened at all, just perfectly
at peace and perfectly comfortable as if this is
where I should be.

—*A Collection of Near Death Research Readings*

You are the light of the world.

Jesus (Matthew 5:14)

. . . this light was so total and complete that you didn't look at the light, you were *in* the light.

—*Recollections of Death*

In the middle of one circle was a most beautiful being. . . . An immense radiant love poured from it. An incredible light shone through every single pore of its face. . . . I was filled with an intense feeling of joy and awe. I was consumed with an absolutely inexpressible amount of love.

—*Heading Toward Omega*

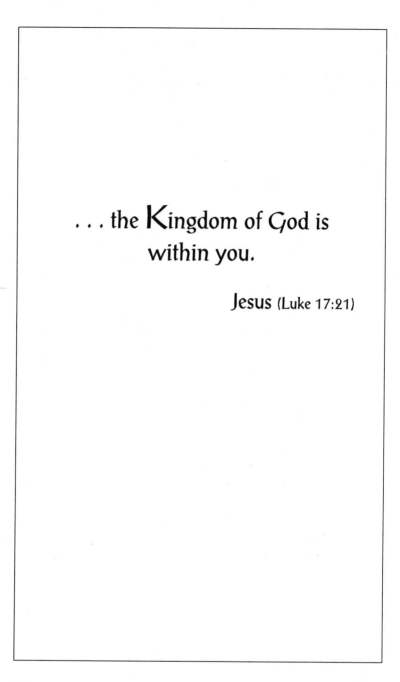

. . . the Kingdom of God is
within you.

Jesus (Luke 17:21)

For what seemed to be endless time, I experienced this Presence. The Light Being, pure, powerful, all-expansive, was without a form. Great waves of awareness flowed to me and into my mind.

—*The New Age Handbook of Death and Dying*

I just found myself in this extremely bright light and felt absolute peace. I feel the light and the peace were one. . . . I had no sense of separate identity. I was in the light and one with it.

—*Return from Death*

I went forward towards the light and as I did so I had such a feeling of freedom and joy, it's beyond words to explain. I had a boundless sense of expansion.

—*Return from Death*

. . . for you are all children of light and children of the day; we are not of the night or the darkness.

Paul (1 Thess. 5:5)

Before my own experience, I thought I understood God. I knew there was no Old Man with a white beard. I had done quite a bit of reading of esoteric material and thought I had somewhat of an idea that God was much bigger than the Old Man and was rather a "Force" of some sort.

During my experience I realized that no matter how large a Force I envisioned, it was still too limited to encompass G O D. I found that it is not possible to imagine G O D, and that it is okay to not know something, to be unable to define (and therefore limit) something. I found that there is so much "out there" that I will get to at some other point during my existence, that even though all knowledge is available, it is available only when we are ready to receive it.

—*Love and God in the Near Death Experience*

The way to God is but one step; the step out of yourself.

Abu Said of Mineh

I seemed to "float" along a corridor towards, then into, all enveloping brightness and light with indefinable shades of pastel-like colours. There were what I can only describe as billions of beautiful shimmering forms, no outlines, as they were all "cloaked" in what looked like a garment of translucent light. The most wonderful thing was the music, which I can only describe as almost a tangible joy from, yet part of and encompassing these forms, of which one appeared to be the source and somehow embraced all else.

I found myself travelling towards this tremendous light, so bright that it would have blinded me if I'd looked at it here, but there it was different. I reached the light which was all around me . . . and I felt this wonderful love enfolding me and understanding me. No matter what my faults, what I'd done or hadn't done, the light loved me unconditionally.

A light was glowing invitingly—I was encouraged by a strong feeling to enter the light. I approached without haste as I felt the light was part of the jigsaw to which I rightfully belonged. As I entered I felt the light glow. I was peaceful, totally content and I understood why I was born on earth and knew the answer to every mystery.
—*Whole in One*

We learn that God IS;
that he is in me; and that
all things are shadows of him.

Ralph Waldo Emerson

There was a person radiating a white light so bright I couldn't make out a body but saw a face, also radiating very white light. . . . Down in front of this being (I could not tell if it was male or female) was a semi-circle with what appeared to be a white bench. Several young people dressed in white were sitting on the bench and looking up at the being. There was no conversation, but I came to understand I could ask or think questions that I most wanted to know and the answer would be given to me. I can't recall anything but my question about how the universe was formed and after (understanding all) thinking it was strange I hadn't thought of it before because it was all so simple. It seemed as if all knowledge flowed from this being . . . I remember being told I had to leave. I didn't want to go and remember asking how I was doing so far. I was told, "Okay, so far" and was urged to leave.

—*Case 51*

CHAPTER 3

Jesus

Truly I tell you, whoever
does not receive the kingdom
of God as a little child will
never enter it.

Jesus (Mark 10:15)

I was trying to get to that light at the end,
because I felt that it was Christ, and I was
trying to reach that point. It was not a
frightening experience. It was more or less a
pleasant thing. For immediately, being a
Christian, I had connected the light with Christ,
who said, "I am the light of the world."
I said to myself, "If this is it, if I am to die,
then I know who waits for me at the end,
there in that light."

—*Life After Life*

The ritual of him who has seen the Shah [truth] is above anger and kindness, infidelity and religion.

Rumi (Mathnawi)

I would say it was Jesus Christ; I mean it looked like him. He was dressed in a robe that was a robin's egg blue, and a long flowing robe that wrapped around him and he had this staff that was a bright gold. It must have been ten feet high. I was looking at him. We were having a conversation. If I could ever put my mind into the space I was in there and know what we were talking about, I'm sure I would really have a lot of satisfactory feelings about a lot of questions that I've been wondering about. . . . (As to the conversation), I can't remember it, but I was really comfortable talking and whatever it was, I agreed with it. There wasn't any unpleasant feelings during the whole experience. . . .

Vision was clear, everything that was there stood out. . . . The colors had a brilliance, this whole person had a brilliance or an aura about him. . . . It was probably the happiest I've ever been.

And as for the skeptics: Going through an experience like that, afterwards it just puts a belief into you that no matter what anybody says or whoever tries to disqualify these, it will never hold up with me because I believe I have seen something of where I'm eventually going . . .
— *Do Suicide Survivors Report Death Experiences?*

The light that never changes,
above the eye of the soul,
above the intelligence . . .

Saint Augustine

He was about eight feet tall, with long hair and a white robe. It wasn't Christ, it may have been an angel, though, taking me to Christ.

—*Childhood Near-Death Experiences*, NDE age 16

Somehow an unexpected peace descended upon me. I found myself floating on the ceiling over the bed looking down at my unconscious body. I barely had time to realize the glorious strangeness of the situation—that I was me but not in my body—when I was joined by a radiant being bathed in a shimmering white glow. Like myself, this being flew but had no wings. I felt a reverent awe when I turned to him; this was no ordinary angel or spirit, but he had been sent to deliver me. Such love and gentleness emanated from his being that I felt that I was in the presence of the messiah.

—*Amazing Grace*

So long as one does not become simple like a child, one does not get divine illumination. Forget all the worldly knowledge that thou hast acquired and become as ignorant as a child, and then wilt thou get the divine wisdom.

Sri Ramakrishna

There was no separateness at all. The peace that I felt was indescribable, it was something I have never known before and I have never been able to reach again, even in moments of meditation or great beauty. I saw my parents approaching me, they appeared as I always remembered them to be. They seemed not at all surprised to see me, in fact they looked as if they were waiting for me and saying, "We've been waiting for you." I know we communicated some things and I believe many things, but I don't remember really what they were. I know that I was in the surroundings of something very beautiful, very spiritual. I can only say that I believe that I was in a state of total cosmic consciousness. I know that I communicated with my parents and with people around me, but it was not in words, it was a form of telepathic communication. I seemed to be told or made aware of telepathically that I would be seeing or talking to possibly someone that I believed to be God or Christ, I don't know. I felt tremendous peace and oneness, the unity was indescribable.

—*Return from Death*

All holy lives are Thine,
O Mazda [God], in truth,
all which have been, which are
and which shall be.

Zarathushtra

In this place I saw people that I knew had died.
There were no words spoken, but it was as if
I knew what they were thinking and at the
same time I knew that they knew what I
was thinking. I felt a peace that passed all
understanding. It was a marvellous feeling.
I felt exhilarated and felt I was one with everything. I saw Christ but the light coming from
Him was so bright that it would normally blind
you. I felt as if I wanted to stay there for ever,
but someone, I felt it was my guardian angel,
said, "You have to go back as you have not
finished your term." Then I felt a kind of
vibrating and I was back again.

—*Return from Death*

He who will drink from my
mouth will become like me.
I myself shall become he,
and the things that are hidden
will be revealed to him.

Jesus (Gospel of Thomas v. 108)

It was white yet golden. For all its brilliance, it didn't hurt to look at it at all. It was pure, strong. It was truth, justice. It was Jesus. I knew this was Jesus the same way I knew I was dead. I just did. The Light came to me, it enveloped me. It was around me, surrounding, supporting me. I floated. I felt no weight, no pain, nothing except pleasure, love. The Light was in me, in between the molecules, the cells of my body. He was in me—I was in him. . . . I knew all things. I saw all things. I was all things. But not me; Jesus had this. And as long as I was "in Him" and He was "in me" I had this power, this glory (for lack of a better word).

—*Case 58*

For everyone who asks receives,
and everyone who searches finds,
and for everyone who knocks,
the door will be opened.

Jesus (Luke 11:10)

I left but stood there wanting to help this poor soul (which was in effect me). [Then] I was on the third level and a voice said "choose." I saw Jesus, the Blessed Mother, and the archangel Michael. My message was un-conditional love; learn to love your family; you love others, but learn to love your family. . . . I had just finished my Master's [degree], but I hadn't taught, or gotten married, or had a family. I was told to choose life.

—*Case 56*

CHAPTER 4

Angels, Spirits, Deceased Loved Ones, and Other Helpers

I am borne away by the mighty
and shining ones . . .

The Egyptian Book of the Dead

There was instead peace and joy and harmony and light. Oh, what a Light it was! As I became increasingly aware of it, it was gold and silver and green and full of love. As the sensations solidified, and this seemed timeless because there was no hurry in this place, I became aware of a being sitting beside me. He wore a white robe, and exuded peace. He was the one who had comforted me during the latter stages of my voyage, I knew instinctively. He was comforting me still. I knew he would be all the friends I never had, and all the guides and teachers I would ever need. I knew that he would be there if ever I needed him, but that there were others for him to look out for, so I needed to care for myself as much as I reasonably could.

—*Amazing Grace*

God is like a mirror.
The mirror never changes
but everyone who looks at it
sees a different face.

The rabbis of the Midrash

After death I went to heaven. It looked beautiful. There were beautiful gardens full of flowers. I saw Yamdoots [Hindu messengers of death], of black complexion. I also saw Yamaraj [Hindu king of death], all black, tall and in robust health.

—*At the Hour of Death*

I was in a very safe place. My stepfather, my real father, and the woman who raised me (who were all dead) were there. What they were saying to me made me feel OK.

—*Case 22*

My grandfather told me to go back and to shape up.

—*Case 5*

The Light was behind me; there were two dark friendly forms beside me.

—*Case 32*

We here respectfully remember
all pious Men and Women
of all the World,
All that are, and were and
are to be . . .

An old prayer of the Magi

. . . three beings who were very, very white and very glowing with bodies enshrouded in this moving gold. One said, "You must go back."

—Do Suicide Survivors Report Death Experiences?

. . . my uncle himself was more vibrant and he was a lot younger.

—Do Suicide Survivors Report Death Experiences?

My father, who had died in 1932, I think it was. My mother was there and she died in 1949. My sister died in about 1970. . . . There was a lot of love. There was love both ways. You knew what was in their hearts. They also told me that I had to go back.

—The Light Beyond

We believe in Allah [God] and that which is revealed to us . . . and the other prophets. We make no distinction between any of them.

Koran (2 : 136)

This time we were audience to a choir of angels singing. Angels were totally outside my reality at the time, yet somehow I knew these beautiful beings to be angelic. They sang the most lovely and extraordinary music I had ever heard. They were identical, each equally beautiful. When their song was over, one of their number came forward to greet me. She was exquisite and I was mightily attracted, but I then realized my admiration could only be expressed in a wholly nonphysical manner, as to a little child. I was embarrassed by my error, but it did not matter. All was forgiven in this wonderful place.

—*Amazing Grace*

. . . the simple yet utterly
inexpressible union of the soul
with its God.

Evelyn Underhill

I could feel this white light around my head and then it started to move over to here where I could see it on the side, and it started talking to me. I was flabbergasted . . . it was my great grandmother who had died maybe a year, two years [before].

—*Do Suicide Survivors Report Death Experiences?*

It was quiet and full of light, and Father was waiting for me. . . . Soon I discovered that we were not talking, but thinking. I knew dozens of things that we did not mention because he knew them. He thought a question, I an answer, without speaking; the process was practically instantaneous. At the same time I caught his question I caught other things in his mind. . . . What he said was in ideas, no words: if I were to go back at all I must go at once . . .

—*A Collection of Near Death Research Readings*

The images are manifest to man, but the light in them remains concealed in the image of the light of the Father.

He will become manifest, but his image will remain concealed by his light.

Jesus (Gospel of Thomas v.83)

The two people with me in the tunnel helped me as soon as I got there. I didn't know where I was exactly but I wanted to get to that light at the end. They told me I would be okay and they would take me into the light. I could feel love from them. I didn't see their faces, just shapes in the tunnel. When we got into the light I could see their faces. This is hard to explain because this is very different from life in the world. I don't have any word for it. It was like they were wearing very white robes. Everything was lighted.

—"The Light Beyond"

The kingdom of God is not coming with things that can be observed; nor will they say, "Look, here it is!" or "There it is!" For, in fact, the kingdom of God is among you.

Jesus (Luke 17:20,21)

There were five or six people wearing garments that were loose and hooded standing about. I remember talking with two in particular while three, possibly four, were standing around me. The warmth of love, feeling of joy and heightened consciousness was so different from anything I have ever known; I don't know how to describe it other than to compare life as I had known it to be asleep, while this was like being awake. It seemed to be what was truly real . . .

—*Case 51*

CHAPTER 5

Judgement
(The Life Review)

You judge by human standards;
I judge no one.

Jesus (John 8:15)

I immediately realized that this being could see right through me and reveal my deepest secrets. . . . His love encouraged me to go through my life up to that point. I saw, relived, remembered things that had happened in my life: not only what actually took place but also the emotions involved. . . . And because of the love and understanding radiating from the being of light, I found the courage to see for myself, with open eyes and without defenses. . . . the being offered me an alternative way to act: not what I *should* have done, which would have been moralizing, but what I *could* have done— an open invitation that made me feel completely free to accept or not to accept his suggestions. . . . I felt totally free and respected. Needless to say, his suggestions were all for a more loving and understanding attitude.

—*Amazing Grace,* NDE age 5

The Moving Finger writes;
and, having writ,
Moves on: nor all your
Piety nor wit
Shall lure it back to cancel
half a Line,
Nor all your Tears wash out
a Word of it.

Omar Khayyam

My life flashed before my eyes and it seemed
like God was there.

—Case 1

I was given the choice to go to the light. I saw
my life (review) of my friends and my Nanny.
I was told I would have to work for it. As an
adult I've wondered what "work for it"
meant. It's always been there (my near death
experience). It comes up again and again at
periods of life—I suddenlybecame very aware
of it. It's part of my very being.

—Case 32, NDE age 5

The One who guides me motions and I understand. I think and it is done. No effort, I make
absolutely no effort. Pictures flash about me,
tears roll down my cheeks. I feel such relief,
such comfort. Some memories of the past come
and I *know*. Understanding floods my mind.
So many thoughts try to crowd into my head, I
can't sort them out. I am tired. All of that is far
away, so long ago.

—The New Age Handbook of Death and Dying

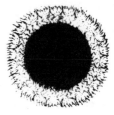

Praise be to Allah [God],
Lord of the Creation,
The Compassionate,
the Merciful,
King of Judgement-day.

Koran (1 : 1)

After all this banging and going through this long, dark place, all of my childhood thoughts, my whole entire life was there at the end of this tunnel, just flashing in front of me. It was not exactly in terms of pictures, more in the form of thought, I guess. I can't exactly describe it to you, but it was just all there. It was just all there at once, I mean, not one thing at a time, blinking off and on, but it was everything, everything at one time. I thought about my mother, about things that I had done wrong. After I could see the mean little things I did as a child, and thought about my mother and father, I wished that I hadn't done these things, and I wished I could go back and undo them.

—*Life After Life*

The heart of Osiris hath in
very truth been weighed,and
his soul hath stood as a witness
for him; it hath been found true
by trial in the Great Balance.

The Egyptian Book of the Dead

When the light appeared, the first thing he said to me was "What do you have to show me that you've done with your life?" . . . He was trying to show me something in each one of these flashbacks. It's not like he was trying to see what I had done—he knew already—but he was picking out these certain flashbacks of my life and putting them in front of me so that I would have to recall them.

All through this, he kept stressing the importance of love. . . .

He seemed very interested in things concerning knowledge, too. . . . He said that it is a continuous process, so I got the feeling that it goes on after death. I think that he was trying to teach me, as we went through those flashbacks.

—*Life After Life*

Do not judge, and you will not be judged; do not condemn, and you will not be condemned. Forgive, and you will be forgiven . . .

Jesus (Luke 6:37)

. . . the light was showing me what was wrong, what I did wrong. And it was very real.

It seemed like this flashback, or memory, or whatever was directed primarily at ascertaining the extent of my life. It was like there was a judgment being made and then, all of a sudden, the light became dimmer, and there was a conversation, not in words, but in thoughts. When I would see something, when I would experience a past event, it was like I was seeing it through eyes with (I guess you would say) omnipotent knowledge, guiding me, and helping me to see.

That's the part that has stuck with me, because it showed me not only what I had done but *even how what I had done had affected other people.* And it wasn't like I was looking at a movie projector because I could *feel* these things; there was feeling, and particularly since I was with this knowledge . . . I found out that not even your thoughts are lost. . . . Every thought was there. . . . Your thoughts are not lost.

—*Reflections on Life After Life*

. . . let your light shine before others, so that they may see your good works and give glory to your Father in heaven.

Jesus (Matthew 5:16)

Instantly my entire life was laid bare and open to this wonderful presence "GOD." I felt inside my being his forgiveness for the things in my life I was ashamed of, as though they were not of great importance. I was asked—but there were no words; it was a straight mental instantaneous communication—"What had I done to benefit or advance the human race?" At the same time all my life was presented instantly in front of me and I was shown or made to understand what counted. I am not going into this any further but, believe me, what I had counted in life as unimportant was my salvation and what I thought was important was nil.

—*Heading Toward Omega*

Love never ends.

Paul (1 Corinthians 13:8)

My near death experience was before Moody's
book came out. When it did I said: "Oh my
God! Mine is pretty classic just like the book."
It was incredibly clear—my life—going through
what happened. There were figures around I did
not know. The white Light was wonderful!
It was just love. I knew my life would be
reviewed. It was just like flipping pages. I knew
I had done things that I was not proud of, but
there was total acceptance. I wanted to stay but
I was told to go back and be loving.

—*Case 48*

The quality of mercy is not strain'd,
It droppeth as the gentle rain
    from heaven
Upon the place beneath: it is
    twice bless'd;
It blesseth him that gives and
    him that takes . . .

William Shakespeare

(The Merchant of Venice)

I saw this life "pass" in front of my "eyes,"
like watching a movie. I felt others' pain, joy,
sorrows. But I also saw all of my other lives
"pass before my eyes" also back to the lifetime
when I just "existed." The creation of this
universe. Reincarnation if you will.

—*Case 58*

During the judgment [it was] like on a Rolodex.
I could feel the person by me. I kept waiting for
the bad to come up, but nothing bad was
coming up.

—*Case 56*

. . . with a certitude which no arguments will ever shake, this sense of the Living Fact, and of its mysterious contacts with and invasions of the human spirit, may assuredly be realized by you.

Evelyn Underhill

I found myself in a corridor. The corridor did
not end. I was not afraid. There was a white
light. Very clear white colors of light. Off to the
side I could see shades of gray. Off to the side I
could see my childhood passing, going left to
right. I thought to myself, "I'm getting
younger." I did not see my adult life. I felt like I
was not alone, but I did not see anybody.

—*Case 53*

CHAPTER 6

After Effects

And now faith, hope, and love
abide, these three; and the
greatest of these is love.

Paul (1 Corinthians 13:13)

[How does the love that you felt in your experience affect your relationship with someone?] It doesn't allow me to do anything purposely to hurt another human being. There can't be any revenge to anything that anybody does to me. . . . Even if that person has hurt me . . . [to hurt them back] goes against unconditional love. I was shown what unconditional love is; I was given unconditional love, and once that happens, you just can't do it, you just can't deliberately hurt another human being.

—*The Impact of a Near Death Experience on Family Relationships*

This unmistakable experience
has been achieved by the mystics
of every religion; and when
we read their statements, we
know that all are speaking of
the same thing.

Evelyn Underhill

I've changed my career. I have a BBA; now I'm studying to be an R.N. Life is more precious to me now. I'm not as materialistic. I thought there was a God before. Now I know there is a God and heaven where things are alright.

—*Case 25*

The Light pushed me back; it was a good feeling. Afterwards I spent two months in ICU. It changed my value system. I now believe in reincarnation.

—*Case 13*

The angels and the prophets will come to you and give to you those things you already have.

Jesus (Gospel of Thomas v. 88)

It would be real nice for them to embrace it . . .
but there will always be that space between a
nonexperiencer and an experiencer. It would be
nice, but that's not reality. . . . I can maintain a
wonderful harmonious family relationship—
very loving, close intimate family life, without
need to dump this on them, and try to get them
into my space. I'm much more relaxed in that.
They need to be where they're at, and I'm
willing to accept them on the level that they're
at now; it really is okay.

It's okay if my husband is an atheist and
doesn't believe in God, it really is okay. . . .
Prior to my experience, no way! I would have
wanted to change them, mold them, manipulate
them . . . to get them on my way of thinking or
doing things.

—*The Impact of a Near Death Experience on
Family Relationships*

All things are in God,
and so depend on him . . .

Baruch Spinoza

I never got wrapped up in family bickering like my brothers and sisters did. My mother said it was because I "had the bigger picture." I suppose that might have been true.

I just knew though that nothing we were arguing about had any real importance. After meeting the Being of Light, I knew that any arguing that went on was meaningless. So when anything like that started in the family, I would just curl up with a book and let other people work out their problems. Mine had already been worked out for me. I am the same way, even now—more than thirty years after it happened to me.

—*The Light Beyond*

. . . the Kingdom of the Father
is spread out upon the earth,
and men do not see it.

Jesus (Gospel of Thomas v. 113)

Now . . . I find that everyone I meet, I like. I very rarely meet someone I don't like. And that's because I accept them right away as someone I like. . . . I don't judge people. . . . And people respond to me in the same way and I think that they can *feel* this [in me].

—*Heading Toward Omega*

. . . I don't fear death. Those feelings vanished. I don't feel bad at funerals anymore. I kind of rejoice at them, because I know what the dead person has been through.

I believe that the Lord may have sent this experience to me because of the way I felt about death.

—*Life After Life*

He that finds God a sweet
enveloping thought to him
never counts his company.

Ralph Waldo Emerson

My father had a near death experience during a cardiac arrest. He had a life review. We had not spoken in seven years. After his near death experience he called me.

—Case 34

It took some time even for me to realize I was consumed with an insatiable thirst for knowledge. Dr. Pat Fenske wrote in the June, 1991, *Vital Signs* newsletter that individuals who are experiencers shift to a higher level of consciousness. This I can relate to 100 percent and this has enabled me to understand why I look at things in an entirely different perspective than most people.

—Case 33

"You shall love the Lord your God with all your heart, and with all your soul, and with all your mind." This is the greatest and first commandment.

And a second is like it: "You shall love your neighbor as yourself." On these two commandments hang all the law and the prophets.

Jesus (Matthew 22.37-40)

Before my experience, I guess I was like most people struggling with a better self-image. But I really *experienced* how precious and how loved I am by God—the light—and I am constantly reminded of that in my daily life. I often think, "If He values me so much (as I experienced it that January day), then no matter what bad thoughts I may think about myself—I HAVE to be a worthwhile person. There's no ifs, ands, or buts.

—*Heading Toward Omega*

My favorite thing as a child was to be alone with God.

—*Case 12,* NDE age 5

The things we now esteem fixed shall, one by one, detach themselves, like ripe fruit, from our experience, and fall.

Ralph Waldo Emerson

I haven't spoken about this in detail to anyone but my family and a few close friends. It seems too personal to share with groups looking for answers to something. I have no answers, only questions. Why did it happen, was there a reason for the experience? Would hypnosis help me recall [all the details of] the conversations with the robed beings or help me remember [all] knowledge given by the being bathed in light? Why did this experience change me so greatly? Why am I convinced this was the most real thing that ever happened to me when logic and common sense dictate it wasn't? Why so many unexplained events since then? . . . The experience left me a changed person but not knowing why, full of questions and still seeking answers.

—*Case 51*

CHAPTER 7

Hell

Even though I walk through
the valley of the shadow of
death, I fear no evil;
for you are with me.

King David (Psalm 23:4)

I was aware of everything: good and evil.

—*Case 24*

"God, I am not ready, please help me." . . . I remember when I screamed [this] an arm shot out of the sky and grabbed my hand and at the last second I was kept from falling off the end of the funnel, the lights flashing; and the heat was really something.

—*Distressing Near-Death Experiences*

I have never believed in hell, I feel God would never create such a place. But it was very hot down there and the vapour or steam was very hot. At the time I did not think very much about it, but in the intervening years I have realized both good and evil exist. The experience has transformed my life.

—*Return from Death*

I am no wench,
but I am thy deeds
— hideous deeds —
evil thoughts, evil words,
evil deeds . . .

The Teachings of the Magi

It was not peaceful, much baggage, much unfinished business. All things are connected. You are not your body, you are a soul; mine was in limbo. I knew I would be in limbo for a long time. I had a life review and was sent to the void. The life review was so disquieting. I saw many different ways my life could have taken. I saw my past life in there and other past lives I was not able to recall.

—*Case 15*

May it come to pass that
the Evil One shall fall
when he layeth a snare
to destroy me . . .

    The Egyptian Book of the Dead

I was in hell. There was this terrible feeling of being lost. It wasn't all fire and brimstone like we were taught. I remember this feeling of coldness. There were other things there whirling about. And there were two beings of some kind near me. I believe one was evil, maybe the Devil. He was the force that was tugging me deeper and deeper down into that awful place. I felt enveloped by dark, black evil. I remember frantically trying to put this two-piece puzzle together. I had to get it done or suffer some terrible, nameless punishment. You don't hear any words, you sense it all. Well, there was no way this puzzle would fit and I remember being in a panic. The other being I'm sure now was Jesus. I remember somehow knowing that He could save me. I tried to shout His name but I couldn't, there was this screaming in my head. Then I felt I was rushing through that black void again. I opened my eyes and my wife and the doctors were leaning over me, telling me everything was going to be alright.

—Return from Death

Alas! when the Uncertain Experiencing of Reality is drawing upon me here,

With every thought of fear or terror or awe for all [apparitional appearances] set aside,

May I recognize whatever [visions] appear, as the reflections of mine own consciousness;

The Tibetan Book of the Dead

Upon reaching the bottom of the pit, I had become conscious of some kind of spirit-being by my side. I hadn't looked at him because I could not take my gaze off the fires of hell, but when I paused, that creature laid his hand on my arm half-way between my shoulder and my elbow to escort me in. At the same moment, a Voice spoke, away above the blackness, above the earth, above the heavens. It was the voice of God, though I did not see Him, and I do not know what He said, because He did not speak in English. He spoke some other tongue, and when He spoke, it reverberated throughout the region of the damned, shaking it like a leaf in the wind, causing that creature to loose his grip. I did not turn around, but there was a Power that pulled me, and I came back away from the fire, away from the heat, back in the shadows of the darkness. I began to ascend, until I came to the top of the pit . . .

—*Beyond Death's Door*

Deliver me from the great god
who carrieth away souls,
and who devoureth filth
and eateth dirt,
the guardian of the darkness . . .

The Egyptian Book of the Dead

The only thing I remember was passing out into blackness and then I saw these red snakes crawling all over me. I couldn't get away from them. I would throw one of them off and then another one would get on me. It was horrible! Finally, I was dragged down to the ground by something and then other crawling things started getting on me. Some looked like red jelly. I screamed and cried out, but no one paid any attention to me. I had the impression there were many other people in the same fix all around me. It sounded like human voices and some of them were screaming. It was reddish black in there and hazy and hard to see, but I never did see any flames. There wasn't any devil, just these crawling things. Although my chest hurt real bad, I remember how glad I was to wake up and get out of that place. I was sure glad to see my family. I never want to go back there. I am convinced it was the entrance to hell.

—*Beyond Death's Door*

I sent my Soul through the Invisible,

Some letter of that After-life to spell:

And after many days my soul return'd

And said, "Behold, Myself, am Heav'n and Hell:"

Omar Khayyam

Time was forever, endless rather than all at once. The remembering of events had no sense of life review, but of trying to prove existence, that existence existed. Yes, it was more than real: absolute reality. There's a cosmic terror we have never addressed. The despair was because of the absolute conviction that I had seen what the other side was—I never thought of it as Hell— and there was no way to tell anyone. It wouldn't matter how I died or when, damnation was out there, just waiting.

—*Distressing Near-Death Experiences*

Be not fond of the dull,
smoke-coloured light
from Hell.

The Tibetan Book of the Dead

These bewildered people? I don't know exactly where I saw them. . . . But as I was going by, there was this area that was dull—this is in contrast to all the brilliant light. . . . they had sad, depressed looks; they seemed to shuffle, as someone would on a chain gang. . . . As I went by they didn't even raise their heads to see what was happening. They seemed to be thinking, "Well, it's all over with. What am I doing? What's it all about?" Just this absolute, crushed, hopeless demeanor—not knowing what to do or where to go or who they were or anything else. . . . They didn't seem to be aware of anything—not the physical world or the spiritual world. They seemed to be caught in between somewhere. It's neither spiritual nor physical.

—Reflections on Life After Life

For where your treasure is,
there your heart will be also.

Jesus (Matthew 6:21)

Suppose that when they had been in these bodies they had developed a dependence on alcohol that went beyond the physical. That became mental. Spiritual, even. Then when they lost that body, except when they could briefly take possession of another one, they would be cut off for all eternity from the thing they could never stop craving.

An eternity like that—the thought sent a chill shuddering through me—surely that would be a form of hell. I had always thought of hell, when I thought of it at all, as a fiery place somewhere beneath the earth where evil men like Hitler would burn forever. But what if one level of hell existed right here on the surface— unseen and unsuspected by the living people occupying the same space? What if it meant remaining on earth but never again able to make contact with it? I thought of that mother whose son couldn't hear her. The woman who wanted that cigarette.

—Return from Tomorrow

CHAPTER 8

Theology

The faith that stands on authority
is not faith.

Ralph Waldo Emerson

My doctor told me I "died" during the surgery. But I told him that I came to life. I saw in that vision what a stuck-up ass I was with all that theory, looking down on everyone who wasn't a member of my denomination or didn't subscribe to the theological beliefs that I did.

A lot of people I know are going to be surprised when they find out that the Lord isn't interested in theology. He seems to find some of it amusing, as a matter of fact, because he wasn't interested at all in anything about my denomination. He wanted to know what was in my heart, not my head.

—*The Light Beyond*

Your religion is where
your love is.

Henry David Thoreau

I feel that church is a bit of a sham. Not God, but the people. They seem to fuss over stupid little things that are really just political. But I belong to a lot of churches. I play the guitar in the Roman Catholic folk group, I'm in the musical group of the Church of Christ, and I play with the Salvation Army. I'm probably Anglican but it doesn't worry me where I am—it's all God inside me.

—*Changes in Religious Beliefs, Attitudes, and Practices Following Near Death Experiences: An Australian Study*

I don't think it [church-based religion] has anything to do with what Jesus was about.

—*Heading Toward Omega*

It was not what I expected. I was a Southern Baptist at the time.

—*Case 14*

The nature of these revelations
is the same; they are perceptions
of the absolute law.

Ralph Waldo Emerson

They say if you're not a Christian none of you
will be able to come in through the eye of the
needle, and all that sort of thing. And I think,
well, I went up there and I saw it and I certainly
wasn't a Christian at the time. So how do they
know? So I can't accept it. I've got my own
beliefs and I try to live my way.

—*Changes in Religious Beliefs, Attitudes, and Practices
Following Near Death Experiences: An Australian Study*

I do not believe in God as taught by religion
anymore.

—*Return from Death*

The True doctrine of omni-presence is That God reappears with all his parts in every moss and cobweb.

Ralph Waldo Emerson

My belief in the power of *The Divine Spirit* has grown, my fear of death has gone. I suppose I could say I'm a changed person. I've lost interest in the church, but feel close to something powerful and divine, and I'm also very aware of this influence on my thoughts and actions. I want to understand. I want to go back with knowledge. As I look back I find it interesting to note that for years I thought that the being bathed in light was *Universal Intelligence.* Not until after reading of other experiences did it occur to me to think of this person as any religious symbol. . . . I've been personally left with a very unpleasant feeling about organized religion, but tolerant of all, knowing they just aren't getting it right but not understanding why I know.

—*Case 51*.

CHAPTER 9

What Is Required
of Us?

. . . and what does the LORD
require of you but to do justice,
and to love kindness, and to
walk humbly with your God?

Micah 6:8

[I was asked] Have you learned to love?
                    —"The Light Beyond"

What did you do with your life?
                    —*Return from Tomorrow*

It's the little things—maybe a hurt child that
you helped or just to stop to say hello to a shut-
in. Those are the things that are most important.
                    —*Heading Toward Omega*

Do not do unto others what would not be good for yourself.

The Teachings of the Magi

. . . it was just my personal intelligence confronting that Universal Mind, which clothed itself in a glorious, living light that was more felt than seen since no eye could absorb its splendor.

. . . there was a reason for everything that happened, no matter how awful it appeared in the physical realm. And within myself, as I was given the answer, my own awakening mind now responded in the same manner: "Of course," I would think, "I already know that. How could I ever have forgotten!" Indeed it appears that all that happens is for a purpose, and that purpose is already known to our eternal self. . . .

I was filled with God's knowledge, and in that precious aspect of his Beingness, I was one with him. But my journey of discovery was just beginning. . . .

We are aspects of one perfect whole, and as such are part of God, and of each other.

—*The Impact of a Near Death Experience on Family Relationships*

Do to others as you would have them do to you.

Jesus (Luke 6:31)

All I know is that it's made all the difference to
my life. It's given me a purpose and a joy. A
determination to help other people. I know I
was sent back because I've got work to do for
God. I now know that there are laws governing
the universe. God does not break these laws,
they are part of his own nature. But when we
transgress these laws, suffering and disease
follow and the only way to reverse this is to
learn to live in harmony with God's laws.

—*Return from Death*

One good deed is worth
ten thousand prayers.

Zarathushtra

I felt as if I had emerged from darkness into light. I felt reborn. I know that I am here for a purpose, which is part of God's plan. I feel I am here to learn God's law and to love unconditionally. Since my experience I am no longer content to live life for myself. My sense of fulfilment comes from developing my potential for the benefit of service to others and in this way I also feel I serve God. Material possessions are no longer important. The real riches lie within.

—Return from Death

One good deed is worth a
whole month of fasting. . . .

Baha'u'llah

The first thing I saw when I awoke in the hospital was a flower, and I cried. Believe it or not, I had never really seen a flower until I came back from death. One big thing I learned when I died was that we are all part of one big, living universe. If we think we can hurt another person or another living thing without hurting ourselves, we are sadly mistaken.

—"The Light Beyond"

That which you have will save you if you bring it forth from yourselves.

Jesus (Gospel of Thomas v.70)

And he said to me, "There are no sins. Not in the way you think about them on earth. The only thing that matters here is how you think."

"What is in your heart?" he asked me.

And somehow I immediately was able to look into my heart and I saw that there was nothing in my heart except love. And I understood exactly what he meant. And I said to him, "Of course." And I felt it was something that I had always known and somehow I'd forgotten it until he'd reminded me of it. "Of course!"

—*Heading Toward Omega*

In everything do to others as
you would have them do to you;
for this is the law and the prophets.

Jesus (Matthew 7:12)

[While I was over there] I got the feeling that
two things it would be completely forbidden for
me to do would be to kill myself or to kill
another person. . . . If I were to commit suicide
I would be throwing God's gift back in his face.
. . . Killing somebody else would be interfering
with God's purpose for that individual.

—*Return from Tomorrow*

This is my commandment,
that you love one another
As I have loved you.

Jesus (John 15:12)

. . . I realized that there are things that every person is sent to earth to realize and to learn. For instance, to share more love, to be more loving toward one another. To discover that the most important thing is human relationships and love and not materialistic things. And to realize that every single thing that you do in your life is recorded and that even though you pass it by not thinking at the time, it always comes up later.

—*Heading Toward Omega*

Conclusions

What conclusions can be drawn from the accounts of near death experiencers? In many ways the accounts speak for themselves. The message is simple and highly repetitious. Anyone who listens to or reads many accounts of near death experiencers hears the same basic theme again and again. Briefly put, the message is:

> *God is Love.*
>
> *We are all connected*
>
> *We are all part of God.*
>
> *God's plan for the Universe may be beyond humanity's understanding, but we are a part of it.*
>
> *Hell is the absence of God.*
>
> *Hell is the land of the self-preoccupied who have shut out the Love of God and others.*
>
> *It is never too late to call out to God, even from Hell.*
>
> *It is never too late to turn to the ones who love you and go toward The Light.*

Hell is the most problematic aspect of the near death experience. Many earlier writers on the near death experience have simply ignored it. Hell is most likely under-reported, as it is hard enough to get people who went to heaven to talk about their experience for fear of public ridicule. Even in the accepting atmosphere of near death experience groups, it takes real courage for people to talk of being in hell especially when they were not rescued immediately.

Greyson and Bush in their article "Distressing Near-Death Experiences," published in *Psychiatry* magazine, note three types of hellish experiences. The experiencers who report a rescue from hell appear to be having a variant of the basic experience. The accounts of hell as more of a void fit the visions of hell described in *The Tibetan Book of the Dead* as a realm of the frightened and lost who when they have overcome their fears, weaknesses, and/or self-absorption will come into The Light. G.G. Ritchie in his elaborate guided vision in *Return from Tomorrow* reported that these souls had only to turn to the Light to free themselves.

The third type of hellish experience is a more traditional vision of hell. Greyson and Bush note that these versions are highly variable in phenomenology. The variability of these, like some of the highly detailed and equally variable accounts of heaven, are infrequent and atypical of the more cosmic and consistent visions of both heaven and hell.

It is noteworthy that the reports of near death experiencers who have wound up in heaven and hell do not follow the lines of belief and doctrine. In this book we have accounts of Fundamentalist Christians and Unitarians in hell and of atheists, Hindus, and Jews in heaven.

Probably the best description of hell is that it is the absence of God.

When it comes to the message of who God is and what is required of us, there can be no doubt that the message universally is consistent.

The Being of Light has many names that fit the religious frame of reference of the beholder. This makes sense and was alluded to in *The Tibetan Book of the Dead*. How else would God be revealed to us? All religious revelation filters through we finite beings who are products of our culture, our time, and our symbolic language. Like the wisdom of *The Tibetan Book of the Dead*, it would seem from the accounts of the near death experiencers that God is interested in what is in our heart and not what is in our creed. It is the love for God and one another that is important. To love others is to love God.

Many near death experiencers have come back disgusted with the religious dogma of their formal religion, but filled with the love for God and others. They reject dogma, but not the teachings of Jesus and the other prophets. They reject religion, but not spirituality.

While scientific investigations of the near death experience helps us understand the details of the experience, the lesson of the near death experience is the essence of the near death experience. The lesson is simply:

Love God.
Love one another.
The two are one and the same for we are all connected.

Epilogue

The Spirit of God is over all the earth,
    and in all things;
It is in God that we live and breathe
    and have our being.

All that is, is God,
And while we are here
There is only one rule:
Never hurt anyone,
And there is only one commandment:
Love one another.

Notes to Chapter 1

1. T.K. Basford, *Near Death Experiences* (New York: Garland Publishing, Inc., 1990).

2. J. E. Owens, E.W. Cook, & I. Stevenson, "Features of Near Death Experiences in Relation to Whether or Not Patients Were Near Death," *The Lancet*, 336 (1990) 1175–1177.

3. Thomas Harpur, "Passage to Paradise," *Maclean's*, 105 (1992) #16, 40–41.

4. Abraham H. Maslow, *Religion, Values and Peak-Experiences*, (New York: Viking Press,1964).

   William James, *The Varieties of Religious Experience*, (New York: Signet, 1901).

5. D. Goleman, *The Meditative Mind*, (Los Angeles: Jeremy Tarcher, Inc., 1988).

6. James, *Varieties of Religious Experience*.

7. E.E. Oxman, S.D. Rosenberg, P.P. Schnurr, G.J. Tucker, & G. Gala, "The Language of Altered States." *Journal of Nervous & Mental Disease*, 176 (1988) p. 401–408.

8. James, *Varieties of Religious Experience*.

9. Goleman, *The Meditative Mind*.

10. George Gallup & W. Proctor, "Adventures in Immortality," *Miami News*, (1982) 7–19, B 1 & 2.

11. *American Psychiatric Association (1980) Diagnostic and Statistical Manual of Mental Disorders* (3rd ed.). Washington, D.C.: Author

12. Maslow, *Religion, Values and Peak Experiences*.

13. J.H. Charlesworth, *Jesus Within Judaism*, (New York: Doubleday, 1988).

   R.W. Funk, *New Gospel Parallels*, (Sonoma, CA: Polebridge Press, 1990).

   H.J. Schonfield, *The Original New Testament*, (London: Waterstone & Co., 1985).

   J.S. Spong, *Rescuing the Bible from Fundamentalism*, (San Francisco: HarperCollins, 1991).

References

"Adventures in Immortality" G. Gallup & W. Proctor, *Miami News,* 1982, 7–19, B 1 & 2.

"Amazing Grace" K. Ring, *Journal of Near Death Studies,* 1991, (10) 11–39.

American Psychiatric Association Diagnostic and Statistical Manual of Mental Disorders (3rd ed.). (Washington, D.C.: Author, 1980)

"At Death's Window" A.S. Genova, *News-Sun Sentinel,* Ft. Lauderdale, FL, 1988, 8–28 p. 1 E +

At the Hour of Death, K. Osis & E. Haraldsson, (New York: Avon Books,1977)

Beyond Death's Door, M. Rawlings, (Nashville, TN: Thomas Nelson, Inc., 1978)

"Changes in Religious Beliefs, Attitudes, and Practices Following Near Death Experiences: An Australian Study" C. Sutherland, *Journal of Near Death Studies,* 1990, (9), 21–31.

"Childhood Near-Death Experiences" M. Morse, P. Castillo, D. Venecia, J. Milstein & D.C. Tyler, *American Journal of Diseases of Children,* 1986, (140), 1110–1113

Closer to the Light, M. Morse & P. Perry, (New York: Villard Books, 1990)

A Collection of Near Death Research Readings, C.R. Lundahl, (Chicago: Nelson-Hall, 1982)

"Distressing Near-Death Experiences" B. Greyson and N.E. Bush, *Psychiatry,* 1992, (55) 95-109

"Do Suicide Survivors Report Death Experiences?" K. Ring & S. Franklin, *Omega,* 1991, (12) 191-208

"Features of Near-Death Experiences in Relation to Whether or Not Patients Were Near Death" J.E. Owens, E.W. Cook & I. Stevenson, *The Lancet,* 1990, (336) 1175-1177

"The Impact of a Near Death Experience on Family Relationships" M. Insinger, *Journal of Near Death Studies,* 1991, (9), 141–181

Heading Toward Omega, K. Ring, (New York: William Morrow, 1989)

Jesus Within Judaism, J.H. Charlesworth, (New York: Doubleday, 1988)

"The Language of Altered States" E.E. Oxman, S.D. Rosenberg, P.P. Schnurr, G.J. Tucker & G. Gala, *Journal of Nervous & Mental Disease,* 1988, (176) p. 401–408.

Life After Life, R.A. Moody, (Covington, GA: Mockingbird Books, 1975)

The Light Beyond, R.A. Moody, (New York: Bantam Books,1988)

"The Light Beyond" R. A. Moody & P. Perry, *New Age Journal,* 1988, (3) 55–67

"Love and God in the Near Death Experience" L. Morabito, *Journal of Near Death Studies,* 1990 (9), 65–66

The Meditative Mind, D. Goleman, (Los Angeles: Jeremy Tarcher, Inc., 1988)

Near Death Experiences, T.K. Basford, (New York: Garland Publishing, Inc., 1990)

The New Age Handbook of Death and Dying, C.W. Parrish-Harra, (Santa Monica, CA: IBS Press,1982)

New Gospel Parallels, R.W. Funk, (Sonoma, CA: Polebridge Press, 1990)

The Original New Testament, H.J. Schonfield, (London: Waterstone & Co., 1985)

"Passage to Paradise" T. Harpur, *Maclean's,* 1992, (105) #16, 40–41

Recollections of Death, M.B. Sabom, (New York: Harper & Row, 1982)

Reflections on Life After Life, R.A. Moody, (Covington, GA: Mockingbird Books, 1977)

Religion, Values and Peak-Experiences, A.H. Maslow, (New York: Viking Press, 1964)

Return from Death, M. Grey, (London: Arkana, 1985)

Return from Tomorrow, G.G. Ritchie & E. Sherrill, (Old Tappan, NJ: Fleming Revell Co., 1978)

The Return from Silence, D.S. Rogo, (Northamptonshire, England: Aquarian Press, 1989)

Rescuing the Bible from Fundamentalism, J.S. Spong, (San Francisco: HarperCollins, 1991)

The Varieties of Religious Experience, W. James, (New York: Signet, 1901/ 1958)

Whole in One, D. Lorimer, (London, Arkana, 1990)

Religious Quotations

Ballou, R.O. (1967) *The World Bible.* New York: Viking Press.

Bode, D.F.A. & Nanvutty, P. (Translators) (1952) *Songs of Zarathushtra.* London: George Allen and Unwin, Ltd.

Budge, E.A. (Translator) (1967) *The Egyptian Book of the Dead,* New York: Dover.

Dawood, N.J. (Translator) (1956) *The Koran.* Middlesex, England: Penguin Books.

Emerson, R.W. (1926) *Essays.* New York: Harper & Row.

Esslemont, J.E. (1976) *Baha'u'llah and the New Era.* New York: Pillar Books.

Evans-Wentz, W.Y. (Translator) (1960) *The Tibetan Book of the Dead.* London: Oxford University Press.

Fitzgerald, E. (Translator) (1960) *The Rubaiyat of Omar Khayyam.* Westwood, NJ: Fleming Revelle Co.

Goleman, D. (1988) *The Meditative Mind.* Los Angeles: Jeremy P. Tarcher, Inc.

Lambdin, T.O. (Translator) *The Gospel of Thomas.* In *The Nag Hammadi Library in English.* (1988). San Francisco: Harper & Row.

Longfellow, S. (1874) "O Life That Maketh All Things New." *Hymns in New Form for Common Worship* (1988). Boston: Beacon Press.

New Revised Standard Version Bible (1989), Nashville, TN: Thomas Nelson, Inc.

Rice, C. (1988) *The Persian Sufis.* London: Allen & Unwin, Ltd.

Shah, I. (1964) *The Sufis.* New York: Doubleday.

Shield, B. & Carlson, R. (Ed.) (1990) *For the Love of God.* San Rafael, CA: New World Library.

Spinoza, B. (1991) *Ethics.* New York: Carol Publishing Group.

Underhill, E. (1914/1942) *Practical Mysticism.* Columbus, OH: Ariel Press.

Zaehner, R.C. (1956) *The Teachings of the Magi.* London: George Allen & Unwin, Ltd.